SPARK

A PEDIATRICIAN'S GUIDE TO REBUILDING TRUST,
RESTORING CONNECTION, AND IGNITING YOUTH
POTENTIAL

ELIZABETH R. HENRY, MD

Manufactured in the United States of America

ISBN: 979-8-9936902-1-6

Price: $19.95

FIRST EDITION –

Photographer: Tinnetta Bell

CGI by Euan Allen

Praise for Dr. Liz's Work

"Dr. Liz is an exceptional communicator whose expertise and compassion shine through in all she does. Just as she has inspired and guided employees at PepsiCo, she provides families with valuable insights and practical tools. Her honesty, warmth, and ability to address difficult topics with ease make her a trusted resource for parents and youth."

—P. Antonio Tataranni, MD
Chief Medical Officer, SVP, R&D Life Sciences
PepsiCo

"Dr. Liz is an invaluable resource for parents and families. She offers meaningful insights that empower young people to recognize their potential while equipping parents with practical tools and clear direction. Her guidance helps families face challenges together, move forward with confidence, and ultimately thrive. I wholeheartedly recommend her to anyone seeking to rebuild trust, restore connection, and ignite youth potential."

—Dr. John Ravally
Superintendent, Franklin Township Public Schools

"Dr. Liz has a unique ability to understand both parent and youth perspectives—a gift shaped by her work as a pediatrician. Her advice, like reminding me that 'you're not raising children; you're raising adults,' has transformed how I approach parenting. Her wisdom and tools help families build accountability, strengthen connection, and grow in confidence."

—Perry Le Blanc
Senior Executive, Financial Services

"After graduating college into the uncertainty of the pandemic, Dr. Liz's work gave me the tools and confidence to move forward. Her insights were thoughtful and engaging, but what stayed with me most were the personal affirmations and the space she created for honest reflection. Her warmth and genuine care made me feel seen, supported, and capable—sometimes you just need the reassurance that you're doing okay and that things will work out if you take control of your life."

—Antoinette R., USC, Class of 2020

"I might be Dr. Liz's biggest fan. She changed both my life and my daughter's. Her guidance gave me the tools I needed when my twelve-year-old was going through a rough patch, and I felt lost. We're still learning and growing, but thanks to Dr. Liz, we're in a much better place."

—Sam S.

Table of Contents

DEDICATION

For youth—

May you be heard, known, and appreciated for your strengths, attributes, and talents.

May you live life to the fullest, recognize your greatness, and know that your presence matters, not just for the future but now.

ACKNOWLEDGMENTS

This book would not have been possible without the love and support of my husband, Keith, and the inspiration of my daughter, Lauryn. Thank you both for your patience, guidance, and for being the wind beneath my wings.

I would like to extend special thanks to Nancy Schwartz Glaeser, Justin Henry, and Genesis Henry for taking the time to review my draft and providing thoughtful feedback.

As always, I appreciate the ongoing encouragement of family and friends as I continue on the path God has designed for me.

INTRODUCTION

A quiet crisis is unfolding all around us. Many young people today feel disconnected, discouraged, and dismissed. Too often, adults don't know how to respond. As a result, a growing gap exists between generations, marked by silence, misunderstanding, and unrealized potential. We say we are preparing youth to lead one day, but what if we empowered them to lead right now?

I wrote this book to help adults and young people respond to the disconnection and hopelessness many young people feel today, so that together, we can rebuild trust, restore connection, and form true partnerships in a world we all share. I'm not just offering ideas; I'm calling for a paradigm shift —a transformation.

Despair, loneliness, and isolation are replacing childhood feelings of joy, wonder, and possibility. We've sidelined youth for too long, and in doing so, we've lost something in ourselves.

To the adults reading: This is a call to reconnect.

To the youth reading: This is a reminder that your voice matters. You are not too old, too young, too emotional, or too late. You are essential to what comes next.

Growing up, my mother encouraged me to be the best version of myself. She made sure I felt supported, seen, and encouraged. I've spent my life doing the same for my daughter, for the families I work with, and hopefully, through this book, for you.

As a pediatrician, I saw firsthand how many young people struggle under the weight of today's world. They deal with peer pressure, bullying, domestic stress, and a constant stream of crises. But I also saw their resilience, brilliance, and capacity for greatness.

This Book Is for Adults and Young People

This book is for adults who care about young people. It's for parents, guardians, mentors, teachers, counselors, youth leaders, and coaches. It's for anyone who wants to support and empower youth to be their best selves.

It's also for young people. It's for the ones who feel invisible and are silent. It's for youth who feel disconnected and overwhelmed. It's for those who know they can make a difference, but are underestimated or uncertain about which path to take. It's for those who aspire to be great but need encouragement when self-doubt arises.

I've wrestled with the concept of this book for years. Most seasoned literary agents, book marketers, and publishers advised me to choose a single audience. They suggested I write either to adults or to youth, or create a separate companion guide. Since adults are more likely to buy books and turn to them for guidance, I wrote my first book, *You Are Not a Bad Parent: A Pediatrician's Guide to Reducing Conflict and Connecting with Your Teens*, for parents.

The book was well-received, but something was still missing. I was speaking about youth, but not directly to them, and that made the conversation feel incomplete.

Years ago, I wrote a guide for teens titled *Living in Your Zone*. It had been sitting in a draft file since 2010. I set it aside because I wasn't sure teens would read it. In doing so, I realized I was making the same mistake I encouraged adults not to make. I was putting youth on the back burner, treating their voices as optional, secondary, or "not ready yet."

So I made a different choice.

This book is not written for adults or young people. It's written with both in mind. Its structure reflects the intergenerational conversation we so desperately need. To truly understand each other, we must communicate effectively. We must listen, learn, and recognize that we see the world differently, and those differences can be our strength.

Who I Am and Why I Speak on This Work

I'm a pediatrician, bestselling author, TEDx and international speaker, and consultant who helps organizations, schools, and communities build stronger, more meaningful connections with the next generation. I provide practical tools and strategies for effective communication and better understanding.

As a pediatrician, I have worked for over two decades at the intersection of medicine, youth development, and communication. I've had a front-row seat to the growing divide between generations. I've witnessed the tension and misunderstandings that arise when adults and young people talk about each other rather than to each other.

Youth feel uncertain about the future and doubtful about making changes that matter. There's growing distrust, disconnection, and uncertainty about the future. I've seen how easily connections break down, but have also experienced how powerful it is when we rebuild them.

My work is all about helping adults, whether they're parents, educators, or community leaders, support young people in ways that are practical, effective, and grounded in trust. I also work directly with teens and young adults, creating safe spaces where they feel seen, heard, and empowered to grow, even when life is tough.

As a speaker and consultant, I aim to bring clarity to conversations that are often emotional or avoided. I express the thoughts people have but don't know how to articulate, and I provide tools to help them move forward with confidence and care.

I earned my undergraduate degree from Princeton University and my medical degree from the University of Pennsylvania's Perelman School of Medicine. I completed my pediatric residency at Georgetown University Hospital in Washington, D.C. I began my career at The Children's Hospital of Philadelphia and later transitioned into private practice in New Jersey.

I'm the founder and CEO of Dr. Liz Consulting, author of the #1 Amazon bestseller *You Are Not a Bad Parent*, and a respected media voice featured on CBS News New York, iHeartRadio, PHL17, and other prominent outlets. I bring insights from the exam room, classroom, and stage to help families, schools, and communities thrive together.

What You'll Learn in This Book

Although I have specific sections geared toward adults and youth, I invite you, whether you're an older adult or a young person, to read the book to the end. Reading the entire book will provide you with valuable insight into how other generations think and perceive the world around them.

If you're older, please share, discuss, and apply the ideas in this book with a young person in your life. If you're younger, share it with your parents, mentors, or a trusted adult, so they can better understand your perspective.

We can't continue to operate in the same paradigm. We have to shift if we want different results—a world that's more compassionate and understanding. We have to try things we've never done before. It will take movement from all of us, young and old, to change the conversation, shift our actions, and create something new.

Inside This Book

This book has four parts:

Part I: Where We Are and How We Got Here

We'll talk about how and why the older and younger generations often feel divided and disconnected. We'll explore the crisis many youth are experiencing, the generation gap, the unique differences between generations, and how we can begin to shift the current narrative about young people.

Part II: Building the Bridge

This section focuses on helping adults bridge the gap. We'll explore blind spots, how to rebuild trust, how to observe and listen without judgment, and how to let go of the need to control while still offering support that truly helps.

Part III: Living in Your Zone: A Guide for the Younger Generations

This part is written for young people. It's designed to empower you in the face of the challenges you're navigating and to offer ways to feel heard, seen, and valued. We'll talk about how to unleash your passion and potential, shift negative mindsets, and expand your network of trusted adults. You'll find practical guidance on how to face fear, get unstuck, explore new possibilities, and move forward. We'll also discuss how to rise above failure, care for your mind and body, and create a personal roadmap for success.

Part IV: Amplifying Youth Voices and Unlocking Potential

The final section creates a new paradigm of intergenerational connection and partnership. We'll explore how youth can be partners in shaping the world we all share. This section invites you to think outside the box to create meaningful partnerships in your life, your community, and beyond.

Notes on Terminology

In this book, I use the terms "youth," "young people," and "younger generations" interchangeably to refer broadly to Millennials, Generation Z, and those younger, such as Generation Alpha. Although Millennials are often grouped with young adults, they hold unique perspectives as the bridge generation between younger and older age groups. The terms "older generations" and "older adults" primarily refer to Generation X and Baby Boomers, as well as individuals from earlier generations.

Notes to the Reader

Because this book addresses both youth and adults, a few key moments are repeated, sometimes with slight variations, depending on the section and the intended reader. Thanks for reading with that in mind.

THE SPARK CONNECTION FRAMEWORK

B efore we proceed, I would like to introduce a simple framework that helps us understand what makes a real connection possible. It's called the **SPARK Connection Framework**.

Each letter in **SPARK** stands for something we all need to feel connected:

- **S — Support**
  Offering help, encouragement, or comfort without trying to fix or control.

- **P — Presence**
  Paying attention. Putting digital devices away and setting aside distractions to listen and be with that person in the moment.

- **A — Authenticity**
  Speaking honestly without trying to be perfect. Respectfully sharing what's true for you and making space for others to do the same.

- **R — Responsiveness**
  Noticing what someone else might be feeling or needing and responding appropriately with care and consideration. Even small actions make a difference.

- **K — Knowing**
  Taking time to understand each other, as well as yourself. Learning what matters to the people in your life and letting others get to know you, too.

These five principles aren't rigid rules or step-by-step instructions. They serve as guides to help rebuild trust, strengthen connections, and ignite the potential in every young person.

SPARK appears throughout this book, not always by name, but as a thread running through the stories, reflections, and ideas. As you read, see if you can spot it.

The framework is not just something adults offer to young people or something young people bring to adults. It is a mutual exchange, a way of building trust, sharing power, and making space for connection, growth, and understanding.

PART I:
WHERE WE ARE AND
HOW WE GOT HERE

CHAPTER 1

ALARMS ARE RINGING

"The death of self-esteem can occur quickly, easily in children, before their ego has "legs," so to speak. Couple the vulnerability of youth with indifferent parents, dismissive adults, and a world, which, in its language, laws, and images, re-enforces despair, and the journey to destruction is sealed." —Toni Morrison, Foreword to The Bluest Eye

The World Our Youth Inherit Isn't the One We Grew Up In

The world young people are growing up in today is not just different from the one we knew; it is almost unrecognizable. They are facing threats we never imagined as children, including school shootings, climate disasters, cyberbullying, the constant pressure of social media, global instability, and the unfolding consequences of the pandemic. Comparing our lives to theirs is like comparing apples to coconuts. While our experiences may not be the same, we often attempt to apply outdated solutions to address modern-day challenges.

A Crisis in Youth Well-Being

We have a youth mental health crisis on our hands. Recent data shows:

- Suicide remains one of the leading causes of death among youth ages 10 to 24. In 2023, the CDC reported it was the second leading cause of death in this age group.[1]

- 18.1 percent of adolescents (ages twelve to seventeen) experienced a major depressive episode in 2023.[2]
- Approximately four in ten high school students reported experiencing persistent feelings of sadness or hopelessness in 2023.[3]
- In 2023, 66 percent of LGBTQ+ youth reported symptoms of anxiety and 53 percent reported symptoms of depression.[4]
- Between 2021 and 2023, nearly one in five adolescents aged twelve to seventeen (19.7 percent) reported anxiety symptoms, and 17.8 percent reported depressive symptoms over the preceding two weeks.[5]
- Nearly one in three US teens experiences anxiety that interferes with their daily functioning. It's the most common mental health condition to affect teenagers.[6]

Data from the *2024 National Survey on Drug Use and Health* show slight improvements in some areas. In 2024, the number of twelve to seventeen-year-old adolescents who seriously considered suicide in the past year decreased from 3.4 million (12.9%) in 2021 to 2.6 million(10.1%) in 2024. The survey also revealed slight declines in suicide planning, from 1.6 million (6.2%) to 1.2 million (4.6%), and in suicide attempts, from 940,000 (3.6%) to 700,000 (2.7%).[7]

The reality, however, remains concerning. In just one year, 700,000 teens attempted suicide. These numbers, though slightly lower than in previous years, still represent an alarming level of distress among America's youth.

In 2021, US Surgeon General Vivek Murthy and organizations like The American Academy of Pediatrics declared a national emergency in youth mental health.[8] [9] We must reevaluate the world we've created for our children. They can't just be kids. They're concerned with far more than "stranger danger." They're growing up in an environment shaped by mass shootings, political unrest, and global instability.

Stories That Say It All

I remember hearing a story about a young boy who didn't want to wear his glow-in-the-dark shirt to school because he was afraid it might make him more visible to a mass shooter. I can't remember where I heard it, but it's a story that has stayed with me.

Wearing a glow-in-the-dark shirt is supposed to be a fun experience, not a potentially deadly one. But for many young people today, school is no longer a secure and safe place. Being hurt or killed in and outside the classroom is a real and valid threat that we can't ignore.

The Climate Crisis Is Also a Youth Crisis

Our changing climate has created unprecedented natural disasters across the US. Wildfires have wiped out communities in California and Maui. Floods have destroyed homes in Texas, New Jersey, Kentucky, and Vermont. Heat waves have sent temperatures soaring in Arizona, while winter storms have knocked out power across Texas.[10]

The majority of the worst disaster years on record have occurred in the past decade.[11] Young people are growing up in this reality, and they are worried about what the future holds.

The Digital Landscape: Connection and Concern

Today's youth have grown up in a digital world that many older generations struggle to understand. Technology evolves at lightning speed, and new platforms appear constantly. Phones are not just devices. They are how young people research, connect, learn, laugh, and express themselves.

Youth use them to access mental health support, stream music, track mindfulness, and stay in touch with distant friends or family. These same tools that provide connection can also expose them to harmful content, cyberbullying, scams, and unrealistic portrayals of life that damage self-esteem and mental health.

A Generation That Feels Disconnected

In 2017, youth aged ten to twenty-five made up nearly one-quarter of the US population. By 2040, that number is expected to drop to about 18 percent, but they will remain a significant segment of our society.[12]

A young adult in her twenties shared this with me:

"We all feel very disconnected as young adults, and we feel like there's no hope for our generation at this point. It's part of the reason why a lot of my friends don't want to have children—they fear putting their kids through similar situations and trauma."

We're Missing the Moment

Youth excitement and energy spark our enthusiasm and curiosity. They ask questions that challenge us to think outside the box. They remind us of who we truly are and what we can accomplish together.

Each generation points fingers of blame rather than working together to create meaningful change. We aren't listening to each other, especially to our youth. We're excluding them from shaping the world they're about to inherit and then blaming them for not caring.

As a pediatrician, I am keenly aware that prevention is the key to unlocking a healthy future. Prevention means responding strategically and thoughtfully to avoid having to react emergently to a crisis. The most effective way to prevent this downward spiral of disconnection, fear, and hopelessness is to invest in our youth.

Young people are our future leaders, healers, teachers, artists, activists, and caregivers. They need supportive adults who are willing to listen, care, and take action. Their resilience and our willingness to respond go hand in hand.

If we continue to ignore their needs, wait for things to change on their own, or expect young people to fix what we've broken, the damage and distance between us will continue to grow. The first step in closing the gap and restoring connection is to recognize the source of the breakdown.

CHAPTER 2

THE GENERATION GAP

"Each generation imagines itself to be more intelligent than the one that went before it, and wiser than the one that comes after it." — George Orwell

A generation usually includes people born over a fifteen- to eighteen-year period. While they may have experienced the same major events growing up, like shifts in society, technology, or the economy, that doesn't mean they all think or believe the same way. People within a generation can have very different backgrounds, perspectives, and experiences. So, using generational labels too broadly can oversimplify just how diverse people really are.[13]

Let's face it. Babies aren't born with beliefs. They're born into belief systems. They learn to see the world through the lens of their family, culture, class, and community. It's natural for parents and society, in general, to try to guide young people based on what they know and believe, but younger generations often question the status quo.

Our differing views and approaches often lead to clashes. Each generation tries to convince the other that their way of thinking is right, when in truth, both views are valid. When we view the world through the lens of our experiences, it's hard to see life in any other way. Real understanding starts with a willingness to view the world through someone else's eyes.

Imagine I'm holding a green coffee mug in my hand. The handle is facing you, and the logo is facing me. If I ask you to describe what you see, you might say, "I see a green mug with a handle." But from where I'm standing, I don't see a handle at all; I see a smooth green surface with a logo. We're both describing the same object. Neither of us is wrong. We're just viewing it from different angles.

The same is true in life. You might see your teenager's friend as irresponsible or a bad influence. Your daughter, on the other hand, sees something different; her friend is exciting, adventurous, and someone who listens to her. To a certain extent, you both are correct. You have different perspectives. So, how do you handle the conflict that inevitably arises?

Ask open-ended questions, show genuine interest, and refrain from judgment. Asking questions like, "Tell me more about your friend?" or "What's fun about being around her?" creates room for authentic conversation, maybe not at first, but eventually. And yes, it's a two-way street. Young people need to understand our perspective as well, but someone has to make the first move. Closing the gap starts with us.

Without empathy and conversation, connection becomes difficult. Let's not view generations as rigid groups, but rather as people shaped by the unique events and experiences of their time.

Given that we still refer to distinct generations, it helps to understand what has influenced each one. That way, we can better see where people are coming from and gain a clearer understanding of their view of the world.

Looking at Life Through the Generational Lens

Baby Boomers (born 1946–1964) grew up during a time of post-war prosperity and the rise of television. While they didn't grow up with the internet, many adapted to digital tools later in life. They value relationships, hard work, and structure.[14] [15]

Generation X (born 1965–1980)—my generation—experienced the rise of personal computers. Many of us were "latchkey kids" who learned independence early. We witnessed the birth of MTV, used rotary phones, and typed school papers on typewriters. We value self-reliance and personal growth.[16]

Millennials (born 1981–1996) came of age during the internet boom and the aftermath of 9/11. The 2008 recession hit just as many were entering adulthood, creating financial hardship and delaying major milestones, including homeownership. They are often described as tech-savvy, purpose-driven, and attention-seeking.[17] [18]

Generation Z (born 1997–2012) has never known a world without smartphones or WiFi. They've grown up with concerns about school safety, rising climate anxiety, and a global pandemic. According to Pew Research, they are the most ethnically diverse and digitally fluent generation yet. They value inclusion, seek meaningful connection, and often push for change rather than wait for it.[19] [20]

Generation Alpha (born 2010–2025) is still unfolding. They are the children of Millennials and are growing up in a hyper-connected, screen-dominated world. According to McCrindle Research, they are expected to be the largest, longest-living, and most culturally diverse generation in history. They're the most digitally connected generation we've seen, and they'll be more mobile, working, studying, and traveling across borders and careers.[21]

Not Just Generations—But Life Stages

Pew Research points out that while thinking in terms of generations can be helpful, it's just as important to consider the person's life stage. A young adult today might be challenging the status quo, not just because they're Gen Z, but because that's something young adults have always done. A middle-aged adult may be balancing care-giving at both ends, not because they're Gen X, but because that's the reality of midlife.[22]

Instead of putting people into boxes, let's consider their background and what's happening in their lives. Each generation might feel like its own "club," but the people in it are more different than we often realize. It's normal for conflicts to arise when one group attempts to impose its way of thinking on another. But if we take a moment to listen and ask questions, real understanding can occur.

I spoke with a mother who was worried about her fourteen-year-old son. He played video games all the time; his grades were dropping, and he seemed distracted and unmotivated. When she tried to talk to him, he replied with one-word answers. She was getting nowhere, so out of fear and frustration, she took away his gaming computer. She also started micromanaging every aspect of his life. She had to know how and when he studied, his strategies for soccer practice and games, and how he spent his free time.

While she thought control would help, it made matters worse because her son had no space to breathe, and there was no room for conversation.

When I spoke with the boy alone, he admitted he felt overwhelmed and needed help managing his time. When I explained his mother's actions to him and asked him to consider the situation from her perspective, things shifted. He realized his mother's micromanaging came from love and concern rather than control.

I told him, "If you start asking for help and sharing your goals, plans, and thought process, you build trust, and with trust comes freedom. When we don't communicate, people tend to imagine the worst."

After that, he opened up and started telling his mom what he was doing before she even asked. His mother later said, "Now my son is managing me."

When communication breaks down, parents often respond by taking over and trying to help. Still, they unintentionally push their kids further away.

What changed wasn't just schoolwork; it was the trust built through honest, open communication. And both parent and child had to meet in the middle to form a connection.

We all have something to teach and something to learn. Let's stop insisting that one side is right. Let's examine the mug from all angles.

CHAPTER 3

REWRITING THE NARRATIVE ABOUT YOUTH

∞

"How much heartache we would save ourselves if we would recognize children as partners with adults in the process of living, rather than always viewing them as apprentices. How much we could teach each other; we have the experience and they have the freshness. How full both our lives could be."—John A. Taylor, *Notes on an Unhurried Journey*

Gen Z as Snowflakes

Young people today want to be heard, seen, and valued for who they truly are. They want to be recognized, not overlooked, for their unique gifts and talents. They are ready to be partners in shaping a better future. The only question is whether we will let them.

That phrase, "whether we let them," is key. Too often, older generations dismiss Gen Z by calling them "snowflakes," assuming they are overly sensitive or emotionally fragile. However, this label, usually meant as an insult, may actually point to something remarkable about who they are.

When you look at a snowflake, you will notice that it is delicate, unique, and beautifully complex. Alone, it will melt quickly, but when snowflakes come together, they create something far more powerful—a snowstorm.

Gen Z is that snowstorm. They are complex and unique individuals who are creative, introspective, and empathetic. Technology connects them to each other and the world in ways we never imagined.

Despite growing up in an era marked by "never seen before" or "first in a lifetime" floods, fires, shootings, and outbreaks, they still fight to be heard, seen, and valued, and continue to make significant contributions to society.

Their empathy, inclusivity, self-awareness, and challenging questions are signs of strength, not weakness. Let's stop underestimating them and start listening. Gen Z is not as fragile as you think. They are a powerful force making a difference right now.

Youth Making an Impact

Gen Zers have made significant contributions already by leading movements and developing solutions, often before they could even vote. Here are just a few powerful examples of individuals who made an extraordinary impact while they were still young.

1. Malala Yousafzai

Malala was born in Pakistan in 1997. When the Taliban took over her region in 2008, they banned girls from attending school. At eleven years old, Malala began blogging anonymously for BBC Urdu about life under Taliban rule and the importance of education for girls. Her advocacy made her a target. In 2012, she was shot in the head by a Taliban gunman on her school bus and survived.[23]

After extensive recovery in the UK, she continued her advocacy on a global scale. In 2013, on her sixteenth birthday, Malala addressed the United Nations, calling for all children to have universal access to education. In that same year, *TIME Magazine* named her one of "The 100 Most Influential People in the World." In 2014, she became the youngest Nobel Peace Prize laureate for her advocacy work. She co-founded the Malala Fund to champion girls' education worldwide and continues to advocate globally for girls' rights.[24] [25]

2. March For Our Lives

Following the 2018 school shooting at Marjory Stoneman Douglas High School in Parkland, Florida, students, including X González, David Hogg, Cameron Kasky, Alex Wind, and Jaclyn Corin, co-founded the March For Our Lives movement, calling for commonsense solutions to reduce gun violence.[26] In March 2018, they helped organize one of the largest youth-led demonstrations in American history, with hundreds of thousands participating in Washington, D.C., and at more than 800 events worldwide.[27]

By that summer, their advocacy had contributed to the passage of over fifty gun safety laws nationwide. It also significantly boosted youth voter turnout in the 2018 elections.[28] Today, the March For Our Lives movement continues as a youth-led initiative committed to addressing gun violence through education, civic engagement, and community-driven action.[29]

3. Marley Dias

In 2015, at the age of eleven, Marley launched the #1000BlackGirlBooks campaign, with the help of the GrassROOTS Community Foundation, to collect and donate books featuring Black girl protagonists. Her campaign has collected over 15,000 books, garnered over 10 billion media impressions, and transformed conversations around representation in children's literature.[30]

She became the youngest person ever named to the Forbes 30 Under 30 list, and *TIME Magazine* recognized her as one of the 25 Most Influential Teens of 2018. She has spoken at the White House and the

United Nations and appeared in national media. Marley is the author of *Marley Dias Gets It Done: And So Can You!* and served as executive producer and host of the Netflix series *Bookmarks: Celebrating Black Voices.*[31]

4. Gitanjali Rao

Gitanjali is an inventor, scientist, STEM advocate, and activist. In 2020, she was named *TIME*'s first-ever Kid of the Year at the age of fifteen.[32]

Gitanjali has leveraged science and technology to develop innovative solutions to some of today's most challenging issues. She invented a lead detection device for water, a colorimetry-based app and device to identify early signs of opioid addiction, and an AI-driven anti-cyber-bullying service. Her workshops and STEM outreach have impacted over 70,000 students globally. Her awards include America's Top Young Scientist, a Forbes 30 Under 30 listing, and the EPA Presidential Award.[33]

5. Sir Darius Brown

In the wake of Hurricanes Harvey and Irma, around the age of ten, Sir Darius created his company, Beaux & Paws. He utilized his passion for sewing to make a positive impact on animals in the shelter. His company donated his handmade bow ties to shelter pets to encourage their adoption. He subsequently formed the PAW-SOME Mission to support shelters with bow ties and volunteers and to raise awareness about adoptable pets. He further expanded his efforts in 2022 by creating "Wag Bags"—care packages filled with essentials for shelter animals.[34]

Through his platform, Sir Darius has helped raise over $500,000. His awards include the Global Child Prodigy Award, the Diana Award, and a personal letter from President Barack Obama. He continues to serve as a national ambassador for pet adoption and animal welfare.[35]

6. Ryan Hickman

Ryan's passion for recycling began in 2012, at the age of three, when he visited the recycling center with his dad. That trip inspired him to collect recyclables from his neighbors, and his efforts expanded to the surrounding communities.[36]

Ryan's Recycling Company is now known throughout Orange County, CA. Ryan has recycled hundreds of thousands of items, been featured on major media outlets, and launched his nonprofit, Project3R, which is dedicated to recycling and environmental awareness. Ryan was a finalist for *TIME*'s Kid of the Year and has received numerous eco-leadership awards, proving that even the youngest advocates can drive global change.[37]

The young people mentioned above offer a glimpse of what's possible when youth are empowered to speak up, take action, and use their unique gifts to create change. They embody the power, purpose, and passion that emerge when young people are engaged in meaningful causes and connected to a supportive community.

You might think today's youth are hard to reach. Many parents worry when their teens spend long hours alone in their rooms or seem more engaged online than in person. So, how do we bridge the gap?

PART II:
BUILDING THE BRIDGE

CHAPTER 4

BLIND SPOTS

When my husband and I travel or attend an event, we often set an intention before we go. Do we want to have fun? Do we want to empower people? It's a game we play.

When we traveled to Europe to celebrate our thirtieth wedding anniversary, we intended to enjoy ourselves, have fun, and create meaningful connections with others. Conversations with people, whether strangers or close friends, can often be superficial, so we wanted to create something different. Not every interaction has to be profound, but when it is, you walk away with pep in your step and more energy. You leave grateful for having had that interaction.

Creating that mindset in Europe made our trip much more enjoyable. We had wonderful conversations with a wide range of people, including hotel staff, servers, fellow travelers, and even a few celebrities.

My experience led me to think more about why it can be so challenging to connect with young people. The answer often lies in areas that we overlook. Those areas are our blind spots.

Blind Spot #1: Focusing on Deficits Rather than Strengths

One blind spot deals with the adolescent brain and behavior. Neurobiology tells us that the teenage brain doesn't fully develop until the mid-twenties. Neural connections in the prefrontal cortex, the area responsible for impulse control, decision-making, and planning, are still forming. The limbic system, which controls reward-seeking behavior and emotions, is also more active during the adolescent period.[38]

Our blind spot is this: Just because a teenager's brain is still developing, it doesn't mean they cannot lead, make decisions, or make a powerful impact. This quote from *The Promise of Adolescence* sums it up best: "The defining characteristics of the adolescent brain are malleability and plasticity. These attributes may sometimes be worrisome, but they also generate unique opportunities for learning, exploration, and growth. Our society needs policies and practices that will help us better leverage these developmental opportunities to harness the promise of adolescence—rather than focusing myopically on containing its risks."[39]

Young people's risk-taking behavior can serve as a catalyst for exploration and new ways of thinking; their impulsivity can spur meaningful change. Their neurobiology is not a detriment; it's just a part of the developmental process.[40]

Blind Spot #2: Preparing Not Connecting

It's natural to prepare young people for adulthood, but sometimes we get so focused on the preparation that we forget that our youth are living life right now. We get caught up in the "doing" and forget just to be present and connect.

Thinking that our role as their parent, teacher, counselor, or mentor automatically guarantees a connection is another blind spot. We need to nurture our relationship with young people just as we would with any other important relationship. They may be younger and less experienced, but they're human beings just the same. They laugh, cry, love, and experience disappointment, apathy, and resignation just like we do, and require the same compassion and understanding. We need to lean in when they pull away and remind ourselves that our youth are human, too.

Blind Spot #3: Independence as a Catch-22

The last blind spot reminds me of the saying, "You better watch what you ask for because you might get it." Older adults want young people to be responsible and independent, but struggle when they start expressing their opinions, questioning authority, and challenging the boundaries set when they were younger. Although it may feel like rejection, the desire for space and autonomy is part of their development.[41] Youth are growing, learning, and trying to figure themselves out.

Our mistake is assuming that young people no longer need us. They need us now more than ever, but just in different ways. Rules and expectations are still essential and should be established, but they should be tailored to the individual's maturity level at the time.

As one mother in my workshop shared, her teenage son once said: "Leave me alone, but don't go away." How insightful was that? Young people need space to explore and room to figure things out on their own, but still need to know you'll be there to support them if and when they fall.

CHAPTER 5

REBUILDING TRUST

It's difficult for young people to trust older generations who have consistently made choices that appear to jeopardize their future. We ignore their voices, dismiss them for their inexperience and naivete, underestimate their capabilities, and then complain when they shut down, shut us out, and don't seem to care.

In their 2018 speech at the March For Our Lives rally in Washington, D.C., X González (then known as Emma González) called out the way young people are dismissed and misrepresented:

"Companies trying to make caricatures of the teenagers these days, saying that we are self-involved and trend-obsessed, and they hush us into submission when our message doesn't reach the ears of the nation, we are prepared to call BS... They say no laws could have prevented the hundreds of senseless tragedies that have occurred. We call BS. That us kids don't know what we're talking about, that we're too young to understand how the government works. We call BS."[42]

After over two decades of caring for young people, I can confidently say that many share the same sentiment. They feel betrayed, alone, and are concerned about their future and the future of this planet. Trust doesn't come back all at once. It's easy to lose and harder to rebuild.

So, where do we start?

A mother once reached out to me about her teenage daughter, who was having a really hard time accepting her parents' divorce. The teen had stopped engaging with school, pulled away from friends, and seemed to be shutting down emotionally. They had been close, but now it felt like they were miles apart. After our conversation, the mom used my first book as a guide.

Things didn't change overnight, but the mother began to show up differently—listening more, reacting less, and practicing greater patience.

Over time, things began to shift. The teen slowly started to re-engage and open up. Her schoolwork improved, she connected with new friends, and by the end of the academic year, she had passed all her classes—something that had once felt completely out of reach.

The mother was relieved to see the progress, but what meant even more was the healing of their connection. The mom rebuilt trust by showing up and being present moment by moment. When young people feel seen, heard, and understood, it opens the door for real connection and growth.

Vulnerability

Most of us say and do the same things over and over again with our teens and then act surprised when nothing changes. If we want something different, we will have to step out of our comfort zone. That's where real connection grows.

You may think you're having a conversation with your teen or young adult, but often it's a one-way street. You're giving advice, instructions, or opinions, but not giving them a chance to respond.

It may not be intentional, but it happens. We all do it from time to time, but when young people don't feel heard, they shut down. They stop engaging and pull away.

It's important to be open and vulnerable, showing your teen that you're not superhuman, and that you, too, deal with challenges, have emotions, and struggle sometimes. Being vulnerable doesn't mean oversharing. It just means being authentic and real.

When I talk with students who feel lost or unsure about their path, I share my story:

Halfway through my first year of medical school, I got completely burned out. I was exhausted, overwhelmed, and wanted to quit. This never happened to me before, so I felt like a failure.

My family and the school administration finally convinced me to take a leave of absence. I soon realized taking a break from the rigor of studying was invaluable because I had the opportunity to rest, travel, and work in other fields of interest. When my leave of absence was over, I was more confident than ever that I wanted to be a physician, and I returned to medical school with more drive, clarity, and focus than I had before. I learned that it was okay to pause, reevaluate, and to make choices that were right for me.

Of course, the story you choose to share will be different from mine. But when you are willing to share times when you had doubts and uncertainties, it creates space for connection. It tells the young person they are not alone and opens up a trusted space for sharing.

Curiosity Builds Trust

One of the simplest and most overlooked ways to rebuild trust across generations is to show genuine interest and curiosity, which demonstrates that you care. Young people can tell when you're just going through the motions. They know when you're more focused on giving your opinion or steering them toward what you think they should care about. When they feel that, they tend to shut down.

When you truly want to know what they think, what they love, and what they're wrestling with, it tells them they matter. You don't have to love what they love. You don't have to understand every trend, song, slang word, or social media platform. If you want to bridge the gap between generations, you have to be willing to step into their world without mocking it, minimizing it, or trying to fix it.

Talking to them about their interests and listening to their concerns opens the door for sharing. If you don't know where to start, some conversation starters are listed below.

- I heard you playing music in your room. Who were you listening to?
- I know you feel we need to be more environmentally conscious. Tell me more about what we can do at home to help the environment.
- What's the best way I can support you right now?
- Do you want my opinion or do you just need me to listen?

Opportunities for Action (Optional)

If you're ready to try something different, here's a simple exercise. It doesn't take much time, and it works whether you're a parent, mentor, teacher, or any caring adult in a young person's life.

1. When you talk to a young person in your life, say something kind, complimentary, or appreciative that you usually don't say, and notice what happens. You might compliment them or tell them you're proud of them. It doesn't have to be big, just something new.

2. *Share a brief story with a young person about a time when you doubted yourself and notice what happens. How did you feel after sharing the story? What was the youth's response?*

CHAPTER 6

PAY ATTENTION

Be a Quiet Observer

Sometimes the most powerful thing you can do is watch. Observation is an important action. It's something you can fall back on at any time and in any place. If you don't know what to say or do at the moment, take a quick minute to stop what you're doing and observe.

To observe is to be intentional about paying attention. You're gathering information not to control or correct a young person, but to understand and strengthen your connection with them.

As a pediatrician, I learned to observe a child's appearance and behavior before examining them. I discovered a great deal about a child's condition simply by looking at them.

Observation gave me clues so that I could focus my physical exam on specific areas. I would watch how patients entered the room. Were they limping? Did they appear sad? How did they interact with their parents? Were they having difficulty breathing? Did they fidget or shut down when certain topics were mentioned?

We all get caught up in "the doing"; life gets busy, and we have a lot of things to accomplish and check off on our to-do list. I remember hearing Eckhart Tolle use the phrase "hurry slowly," and it really stuck with me. At times, you can learn more from slowing down and observing than having long conversations.

Observation requires noticing body language, reactions, expressions, and interactions with other people and the world around them. It might be challenging at first, but you can start by observing from the viewpoint of a stranger who is trying to learn what makes that young person tick. What makes them laugh? Do they move slowly, or do they jump from one activity to the next? How do they interact with others? How do they speak when they're relaxed and when they're upset?

Your Inner Voice

Paying attention isn't just about observing others. It's also about observing yourself.

Every human being walks around with constant inner dialogue, a kind of background noise that comments on everything. We all talk to ourselves. It's how we're wired.

You often see it in movies and TV shows when a character doesn't speak out loud, but you hear their thoughts in a voice-over. The actor stares out a window, and you hear what they're thinking—their opinions, fears, judgments, and regrets.

You have the same inner voice that narrates your life. It comments on everything, including your likes and dislikes, what the young person in your life should be doing, and what you wish you could say out loud but don't.

This inner voice is so automatic that most of the time, you don't even realize it's there. It shapes how you feel, speak, and react, especially when emotions run high.

Let me give you an example from my own life. My daughter moved back to New Jersey for a few months during the pandemic. She had just graduated from USC and came home before Thanksgiving, planning to stay through February since everything was remote. One day, she told me she was planning to switch over her driver's license and officially become a California resident.

When she said that, I became tense and told myself, *I shouldn't have let her go to school out there. I knew this was going to happen. People told me she'd stay on the West Coast. What was I thinking?* My mind went into overdrive. And without realizing it, my tone shifted.

I told my daughter, "I don't know why you're doing that now," in a sharp, annoyed voice. My daughter looked at me and said, "Why do you sound so angry?" When she said that, I stopped in my tracks because I realized what was happening.

I wasn't angry; I was sad because I'd miss her. And I was frustrated with myself for encouraging her to apply to schools in California in the first place.

If I had let that inner voice take charge, it could have created a lot of unnecessary tension between us. I would have stayed annoyed without really knowing why, and she would have continued feeling confused and hurt by my reaction. Over time, that kind of unspoken tension builds walls instead of bridges.

Instead, I told her the truth and said, "I'm not mad at you. I'm just sad because getting a California license means you plan to stay out there for a while. It feels more permanent." Admitting that shifted everything. The tension eased, and we felt a deeper connection.

It's natural to have these inner reactions. We all do it. Noticing your internal dialogue interrupts the parade of thoughts marching in your head and gives you the space to choose your response instead of re-acting from fear, frustration, or sadness. Being attentive also en-hances your ability to listen powerfully and in different ways.

CHAPTER 7

LISTEN FOR THE GOLD

Sometimes you can learn more from what a person doesn't say. A young person might say something that feels dismissive or sarcastic, but if you listen closely, you might hear something else underneath. I refer to that "something" as the gold. The gold is what's buried beneath the surface-level words. It's the fear, doubt, and emotion that they don't know how to communicate.

A mother shared a conversation about her daughter who had been distant for weeks. Their encounter consisted of short answers, eye rolls, and slammed doors. But one night, instead of pushing to find out what was wrong, the mother sat nearby without saying a word.

After a while, the teen started talking about how behind she was in school. The girl felt she was a disappointment because she was failing.

The mother didn't fix anything but just listened, and in doing so, she heard the gold. You can't hear the gold if you're interrupting, correcting, or forming your response while they're still speaking. You have to embrace the silence.

Embracing the Silence

We often avoid silence. We reach for distractions, such as putting in earbuds, turning on the TV, or engaging in small talk. Sitting in silence with another person can feel awkward, but silence is often a useful and necessary tool.

Have you ever looked forward to being with another person? Perhaps you haven't seen a friend or family member for a while and are excited about being in their presence. You've talked to them over the phone or on Zoom chats, but you miss being with them. You wouldn't even mind sitting in silence because being together is all that matters.

Silence is valuable. You'll gain a lot by embracing the silence that arises between you and your young person. Being with a teen or young adult can be powerful if you take the time to savor those moments when you're together and not saying anything. Silence creates a space for ideas and new conversations to arise.

Your teen may be working on their homework or texting their friends. You may be working on your computer. There's no need to force conversation or ask questions. You don't need to do or say anything. Just share the same space and be available to talk if your teen desires to do so.

Space and Grace to Feel

When a young person tells us they're sad, overwhelmed, frustrated, or disappointed, our first instinct is usually to help them feel better.

We say things like, "It'll be okay. It's not that bad. You'll feel better tomorrow." We want to ease their pain, reassure them, or help them move on.

However, sometimes those comforting phrases have the opposite effect, and they can make them feel dismissed rather than heard. They need someone to give them the space to speak freely and the grace to feel what they feel.

Allowing youth to experience their feelings will help build trust and strengthen your connection with them. When they feel heard, it opens the door for more frequent sharing.

You don't have to say much. Saying less is often more. Something as short as "That sounds really hard," or "I'm so glad you told me," can go a long way in validating their experience and knowing that you heard them.

Try this:

In your next emotional conversation, be present, listen attentively, and give them permission to express and share their emotions. Create space for them to express their feelings and see what happens.

CHAPTER 8

CONNECTION OVER CONTROL

Being Present

It may seem counterintuitive, but you have to disconnect to connect. We have a lot on our plates—working, managing family activities, volunteering, spending time with our spouse or significant other, preparing meals, running errands, thinking about tomorrow, next week, and next month, planning, strategizing...you get the idea. We get caught up in the "doing" of life and rarely stop to "be" and experience the moments we share with youth.

Being present means that when your kids say, "Look at this!" or "Listen to this!" you see what they're showing you or hear what they are saying, without thinking about your to-do list. It means focusing on them without checking your emails during the conversation, and giving them and their interests your undivided attention, if just for a few minutes.

Being present means knowing when you don't have much time and saying, "That's great. I look forward to hearing all about it. Let's wait until I finish writing this email so that I can give you my full attention." It means being grateful for the time you spend together and connecting in a meaningful way, without trying to fix or change anyone. It means accepting each other for who you are at that very moment.

When you are present, a new space of vulnerability, openness, love, and trust arises. This space starts very small, like a barely open door, but the more you practice, the bigger that space becomes and the wider that door opens.

It's simple, but not easy, and takes practice—a few helpful strategies are listed below.

1. Use a power word. When you catch yourself thinking about other things, say this word to yourself to interrupt your stream of thoughts. You can choose any word or short phrase. It could be *"here," "now,"* or your child's name. My word is *"be present."* Whatever you choose, use it as a reminder to stay present when your mind wanders.

2. Write three to five things you are grateful for. Taking a moment to be grateful refocuses your mind and brings you back to what matters most.

3. Take five to ten minutes out of your day to stop and pay attention to your senses. What do you see, hear, smell, taste, and feel? What colors do you see around you? Do you hear the birds chirping? Do you smell the aroma of coffee or rain in the air? When you're eating your food, what spices do you taste, and what are the textures? Take notice of the ground as you walk to the car.

We often move from one activity to the next without appreciating the world around us. Taking the time to notice the world around you will center you and bring you back to the present moment.

4. Take five to ten minutes out of your day to meditate or do breathwork. Mindfulness exercises are powerful ways to strengthen your ability to stay present. There are a number of meditation apps available. Focusing on your breath can also make a difference. Breathing happens automatically; we rarely notice it. But when you slow down and pay attention to each breath, it quiets the noise. Your mind has a harder time drifting when you're focused on breathing.

Let Go of the Rope

Sometimes you just have to let go of the rope.

You can have power without force. Take, for example, Dr. Martin Luther King Jr. He was powerful through his words, his character, and his leadership of the nonviolent civil rights movement.

True power lies in being confident in who you are and utilizing your gifts to create positive change. Letting go of the rope is an expression of that power because you are choosing connection over control and responding with strength rather than force.

I have a daughter in her twenties. We have a very close relationship now, but it was a battle of wills when she was a teen. I was a straight-A student as a child and thought my daughter would care about grades as much as I did. Boy, was I wrong.

I remember attending a seventh-grade parent-teacher conference, expecting to receive a good report because she was consistently earning A's and B's. I thought, *This is going to be a good night of meeting teachers, asking questions, and getting glowing reports.*

Then her science teacher said, "Unfortunately, Lauryn is close to failing because she got a zero on a major assignment she never handed in." My husband looked at me quickly, knowing I was trying to stay calm. I could hardly breathe. I said, "Oh, really! Well, can she still hand it in for partial credit?" The teacher said, "Yes." I was livid.

My daughter wasn't with us, so when we returned home, I drove her back to the school to get the books she needed from her locker. She finished the assignment that night and handed it in the next day.

That was one of many moments when I began to learn the hard way that she is not me. She did her best in the subjects she loved, like art and language arts, and would coast through science and math with C's if she thought I would allow it.

The arts were her passion, and the rest simply weren't. Once I recognized that my daughter had her own voice and unique gifts, we stopped butting heads, and our relationship began to strengthen. Letting go of the rope doesn't mean you're surrendering or settling for mediocrity. It means you stop digging your heels in to reconsider your position; you pause to consider that there may be another way.

I spoke with a dad in a similar circumstance. He and his son were at odds, and both were holding on tight to being right. When I suggested that he let go of the rope, the tension eased, and their relationship began to heal. The dad stopped pulling and started listening.

Our role as parents and trusted adults is to recognize and nurture the unique gifts that each young person possesses, even if they are unlike our own. Sometimes you have to let go of the rope.

PART III:
LIVING IN YOUR ZONE—A GUIDE FOR
THE YOUNGER GENERATIONS

CHAPTER 9

THIS PART'S FOR YOU

∞

Introduction

If you're a teen or young adult reading this, I'm glad you're here. This section sat in a folder on my computer for years because I wasn't sure if you would read it. I started doubting myself and questioned whether my thoughts on paper would make a difference, given that you're accustomed to short videos and high-quality graphics. If you're an older adult, please note that I'm addressing the youth directly in this section, but I highly encourage you to read this part as well. The more we understand each other, the stronger our relationships become, and the more we all thrive.

Let's get started...

As young people, you've got a lot going on with school, work, friends, extracurricular activities, and responsibilities. Sitting down to read might not be your first choice, but I wrote this section to help you navigate life's challenges. My goal is to share what I've learned from my own life and from working with thousands of young people, to support you in becoming the best version of yourself.

I want you to feel seen, heard, and valued for exactly who you are, right now. You have something powerful and unique to offer this world. Use this book to support you in unlocking it.

CHAPTER 10

LIVING IN YOUR ZONE

What does that mean, exactly? It means living life to the fullest, giving it your best effort, and discovering your purpose. It means fully expressing yourself and connecting with others, making a difference, being real, respecting others, and honoring your commitments.

Your zone isn't a particular place or location; it's a state of mind. It's that moment when you block out everything around you because you're focused on what you're doing. We often experience being in the zone when we're doing something we love. We become so absorbed in it that for a while, nothing else matters. You're in *your* zone.

Notice I've used the term "your zone" instead of "the zone." We often hear about athletes getting in the zone before a game, or people saying they're getting in the zone before a big presentation. I've made the phrase more personal because everyone has a different zone. Your zone is different from mine. We each have our own space that brings us peace, fulfillment, and joy when we're in it.

You were born with gifts and talents. You can choose to use them or ignore them. Sometimes it might feel like you have nothing to contribute, but that's just not true. You have at least one thing deep down that you know you're good at. It might be playing an instrument, throwing a baseball, singing, reading, or doing math. It could be styling hair, fixing a car, or giving advice.

Whatever it is, that talent is yours. And it's up to you to develop it.

CHAPTER 11

FREE YOUR MIND

Fear can stop everything. You may have many fears, including fear of failing, succeeding, being disliked, not being good enough, or being unloved. Fear can hold us back from our biggest dreams.

There was a time I didn't realize how much fear was running the show. I didn't audition for a college a cappella group because I was afraid of being rejected. I chose not to study abroad because I was scared of the unknown. I didn't invite many friends over when I was growing up because I was worried my house wasn't as nice as theirs.

Fear is supposed to protect us. It's part of our survival system and kicks in when we're in real danger. However, fear can sometimes creep into situations that have nothing to do with survival. It causes stress, anxiety, and regret, and keeps us frozen. It doesn't just throw us off our game; it takes us completely out of the game. Fear keeps us stuck, small, and in our heads.

One of my favorite movies is *The Matrix*, so of course I'm going to quote Morpheus and say, "Free your mind."[43] Free your mind from doubt, guilt, anxiety, and shame. Free your mind from the past, the things you did wrong, and the people who did you wrong. Let all of that go and move forward to express the real you—that version that wants to make a difference and has something to share with others.

So, how do you free your mind? You listen to the voice inside that tells you what you *can* do rather than the one that tells you what you can't do.

To soar to great heights, you have to leap out of your comfort zone. We often keep waiting for the leap to feel safe, but that day will never come. You'll stay frozen if you wait for fear to disappear. Fear doesn't go away; you just stop letting it run your life.

CHAPTER 12

MUTE THE CHATTER

Mute Your Chatter

We are often our own worst enemies. We all have an inner critic, a voice that tries to hold us back from becoming our best selves. The key is to recognize when that voice shows up and not accept it as the truth.

That negative voice isn't going to disappear. Even now, as I write these words, my inner voice is saying, *You have the nerve to write a second book? Who do you think you are, Maya Angelou? You're just a pediatrician. Stay in your lane.* But that voice doesn't get the final say. I recognize it's expressing fear, not fact.

It's a distraction trying to pull me away from my mission to support parents, empower young people, and bridge the generation gap.

Your inner voice might sound like this:

- *"Being MVP was a fluke. It was just luck and coincidence."*

- *"You're not smart. You only got an A because your class is full of underachievers."*

- *"You only got that job because no one else applied."*

- *"You're just lazy. You'll never catch up."*

Sometimes that voice isn't entirely wrong. You may not be doing well. Perhaps you are behind or have failed a class, but putting yourself down doesn't help. I've been there.

I was eight years old and in the third grade, and the class knew me as the "smart kid." One day, the teacher asked, "Who was the first president of the United States?" I raised my hand confidently and said, "Abraham Lincoln!" As soon as I answered, I knew I had messed up. The whole class laughed because the answer, of course, was George Washington. Tears welled up. I shrank down in my seat. I felt embarrassed and wanted to disappear.

But when I look back, I was upset more with myself than with the reaction of the other kids. In that moment of embarrassment, I told myself, *You always mess up. You're not good at this. People don't want to hear you,* and right there and then, I made the decision that I would never speak up like that again. And from then on, I started silencing myself. I wanted to speak and had a lot to say, but fear would always stop me from being my true self.

Don't listen to the voice that drags you down. Listen to your inner voice that lifts you and reminds you that you can still succeed, no matter what life throws your way.

Mute the Outside Noise

Sometimes your inner voice is not the issue. The outside noise from the digital world can be confusing and lead you astray. You're constantly being told what to wear, what to believe, who to follow, and how you should live. The nonstop scrolling of opinions, trends, advice, and comparisons on social media can be exhausting and draining. And with so much information coming at you from around the world, it's hard to know who to trust or what's important.

Of course, social media and online connections have their benefits. You can discover new ideas and learn new skills, like mindfulness, fitness routines, or art techniques. You can stay updated on current events, connect with friends and family, and collaborate on group projects.

But it's also important to disconnect so you can connect more deeply in real life. Participating in non-digital activities, such as playing board games, going on walks, cycling, or simply discussing your day, can strengthen relationships, especially those with your parents and other trusted adults.

When you mute the outside noise, you give yourself space to think and to figure out what *you* believe, what *you* enjoy, and what *you* want to stand for. You create room to explore new interests, develop your own opinions, and build a support system of people who truly know you and have your back.

CHAPTER 13

ASKING FOR HELP

Your support system is critical. You need to build a circle of trusted adults around you to guide you during challenging times. It's important to ask for help and guidance when you need it. Notice I used the word *"when"* because you will need help at many points in your life. Everyone needs help. The most successful people are those who aren't ashamed to ask for what they need.

Surrounding yourself with people who are positive and encouraging is essential. Don't be afraid to connect with individuals from different backgrounds and age groups. You need people with a variety of skills and experiences to support you in achieving your goals.

If someone inspires you, ask them if you can discuss what they do and how they achieved their success. Reach out to them when you need support. Mentors can help guide you through life's challenges, especially if they're working in a field or doing something you hope to pursue one day.

When you create that circle of adults around you, look to them for advice and guidance. Your parents might not always say things the way you want to hear them, and they may not have all the answers. But often their advice comes from a place of love and desire to see you become your best self.

You can find quick answers online, but those answers are not always accurate or helpful to you. Your trusted circle serves as a valuable resource, providing you with real-life experiences, honest feedback, and support from people who know you and genuinely care.

Try This:

Make a quick list of three people who already support and encourage you. Then list one person you'd like to get to know better. What's one small step you could take to build that connection this week?

CHAPTER 14

LOVE THE NO'S

When I was a teen, I hated hearing the word "no." But later, I learned the more "no's" you get, the closer you are to a "yes."

I don't mean wearing down your parents or your professor until they finally give in. I'm saying, don't avoid asking a question because you think the answer might be "no."

Questions are good, so keep asking them. If the answer is "no," don't take it personally. "No" usually means someone can't or doesn't want to say yes at the moment. It doesn't necessarily mean they don't like you, don't care, or that your idea is bad. It just means "no" right now.

Notice I said it means "no" right now. It doesn't always mean "no forever." There are no guarantees that the answer will change in the future, but it's possible. The more you learn to embrace the word "no" with grace, the easier it becomes to ask for what you want without being afraid of the answer.

CHAPTER 15

FLIP IT

"Don't let the circumstances define who you are. Let who you are and what you want to accomplish in life determine how you respond to the circumstances." —Dr. Liz

Life has its ups and downs and may not always go the way you want, but you can shift how you view and respond to the situation; you can flip it. It's not about pretending everything is okay when it's not. It's choosing to see your circumstances in a new way. You can either stay stuck in fear, disappointment, or frustration, or you can move forward.

Suppose you fail a test. Instead of feeling guilty, disappointed, or upset, ask yourself what you could do differently the next time. If someone purposely insults you or says something negative, you have two choices. You can internalize what they say or flip the script by realizing their comment revealed their insecurities, not yours. If they continue being insulting, you might want to reconsider hanging out with them; you need people in your circle to encourage your light to shine.

CHAPTER 16

SHINE

"Nothing can dim the light that shines from within." —Maya Angelou

You deserve to be surrounded by people who allow you to shine, who support your dreams, and who celebrate your uniqueness.

Here's a real example of what that kind of self-expression and confidence can look like, even at a young age.

My daughter wrote this essay at the end of fifth grade. She's now a young adult, and with her permission, I'm sharing it here. I've made a few minor edits for clarity.

"Every day when I choose what I'm going to wear, I choose a style that's all my own. For example, I will mix and match colors, patterns, and fabrics. One time I went to school in a black and orange jersey with blue jeans and a white scarf. No one dared or forced me to wear it on that day. I decided to.

I stepped on the bus, not caring what people were saying about it. I stepped into the school, not caring who was staring at me. But when I walked into the classroom, someone ruined my not caring mojo. They called me over to their desk and said, 'Lose the jersey or lose the scarf. You cannot work them both.' But I simply said, 'Don't tell me what to wear.'

After that, she never told me what to do with my outfit again. Putting together that outfit and walking through the school with a scarf and

a jersey had taken a lot of self-esteem. Self-esteem means having confidence in yourself and your beliefs. Self-esteem is very important because without it, your life will end up miserable."

The essay reveals what it looks like to shine —to be yourself, even when someone tries to dim your light. If we waited for praise or recognition for everything we do, we'd be waiting a long time.

Letting your light shine comes from within. It's not about popularity, perfection, or being the best. It's about showing up as your authentic self. Everyone has a unique talent, and it's up to each of us to discover it.

Your natural talent is typically something you excel at and enjoy doing; it's your passion. When you use your gifts, you don't mind staying late or going the extra mile, and you aim for greatness, not just "good enough." Sometimes your distractions aren't just forms of procrastination but can serve as clues to the gifts designed for you to share with others.

Take my daughter, for example. She would spend hours making short films, building her AP art portfolio, arranging music for her a cappella group, and rehearsing for the school musical.

But spending that same energy on science homework? Not a chance. Her passion wasn't science; it was art. Now she's carving out her path as a singer, performer, songwriter, and producer, turning her creativity into a career she genuinely loves.

You weren't born to hide. You were born to shine. So don't wait for permission. Own your gifts. You get to decide who you are and how brightly you shine. You have the power.

CHAPTER 17

PLUG INTO YOUR POWER

You may feel powerless at times, but you do have power; you just have to plug into it. Most people equate power with force, but they are not the same.

Force takes a lot of effort. It implies resistance, like someone pushing back. True power is the ability to be confident in who you are and to use your talents to create change that positively impacts your community. Some of the most nonviolent people in history were also the most powerful.

Dr. Martin Luther King Jr. and Mahatma Gandhi didn't use force. They used their words, values, and vision to lead nonviolent movements that changed the world. Although they encountered violence and verbal confrontations, they chose to be peaceful. That's real power.

You have the power to choose how you respond to the world, no matter what challenges come your way. We react to everything—to the news, to what people say, and to what people do. When someone pushes our buttons, our reactions often come quickly without any thought; they're automatic. Pausing to choose how you respond rather than react is a sign of true power. Be still, even if it's just for a few minutes. Be quiet and take long, deep breaths to center yourself, calm your mind, and choose your response to plug into your power. When you discover your power, it empowers you with the strength and confidence to speak up.

Try This

- *What's one issue, cause, or situation where you feel called to make a difference, big or small?*
- *What's one step you could take this week to plug in to your power?*

CHAPTER 18

RAISE YOUR VOICE

Speak Up

In this case, raising your voice doesn't mean speaking louder. It means speaking up to share your thoughts, ideas, and opinions. Malala Yousafzai is an example of a teen who raised her voice. She refused to stay silent and spoke out against the Taliban's ban on educating girls.[44]

When she was fifteen, she was shot in the head by the Taliban for her beliefs, but continued to speak up after she recovered. She became the youngest person ever to win the Nobel Peace Prize and continued her advocacy work into adulthood.[45]

She demonstrates how you can create change and make an impact at any age. You don't have to wait until you reach adulthood to find your voice or contribute to others.

Share What's Going on with You

Raising your voice also means communicating more with your parents and other trusted adults in your life. Believe it or not, sharing about your life is often more beneficial to you than to them.

Older adults aren't always asking questions to be nosy. They ask because they care. Their questions are often a way to ensure you're on the right track and to verify that they're doing their part to support you in achieving success, happiness, and overall well-being.

When you don't share much, adults tend to worry. Worry can lead to more questions, frustration, and tension.

When parents or caregivers feel unsure about what's going on in your life, they may start micromanaging or trying to control everything. They're not trying to punish you. They're trying to ensure your safety. One of the simplest ways to take back control is to start talking.

Based on the questions your parents usually ask, you already have a good idea of what they want to know. So take charge and offer that information before they ask.

The more they know, the less they'll feel the need to ask. When you keep them in the loop, they begin to understand how you think, and that builds trust. Over time, they'll see that you're capable of handling more on your own.

Try it and see what happens.

CHAPTER 19

GIVE IT AWAY

Don't hold on to your talents. The more you use your unique gifts, the more they grow. And as you grow, people will begin to recognize and appreciate your skills and passions.

Volunteering is a powerful way to utilize your talents to make a positive impact on both others and yourself. It builds your self-esteem, lifts your spirits, and reminds you that what you do matters. When you focus on helping others, you stop thinking so much about yourself and your situation. It shifts your energy.

Don't keep your talents to yourself. Give them away, and you'll find your light will burn brighter than ever. When that happens, you'll have room to add more spice to your life.

CHAPTER 20

SPICE IT UP

Spice up your life. Don't do the same thing over and over. The only way to discover what's out there is to explore, try something new, and step into the unknown.

Learn something new or try something different. If you think you're not creative, consider taking an art class or a dance class to shake things up. If you do the same thing every day, it gets boring. Change it up.

Don't be afraid of making mistakes and taking risks—the good kind. Join a new club. Volunteer to lead something. Learn a new skill. That's how you figure out what you're good at and what excites you.

Don't let fear of what people think stop you. As Benjamin Mee says in the movie *We Bought a Zoo*, "Sometimes all you need is twenty seconds of insane courage...and I promise you, something great will come of it."[46] So go ahead and spice it up.

CHAPTER 21

CREATE YOUR ROADMAP

The Labels We Carry

You were born with a blank slate, full of possibility. Then life happens.

After you're born, people start labeling you—big, small, smart, stupid, clumsy, athletic, tall, short. Over time, you begin to take on those labels. You even make up some of your own. You may start to believe they're true, even when they're not. Some labels might describe parts of you, but they don't define who you are.

Just because you're not as quick as your classmates in math doesn't mean you're bad at it. You may need to work harder to get the same grade. That doesn't make you a loser. There are other things you're good at. You have to find them.

Understanding Your Parents' Point of View

Most parents want you to be successful and happy, but their idea of success may differ from yours. It can be scary when their kids want to pursue passions with uncertain paths.

Parents try to use their life experience to guide you and protect you from learning the hard way. You want to experience life for yourself; they want to shield you from the pain.

If you understand your parents' perspective, you'll realize they are afraid of letting go, and they want to do everything in their power to prepare you for your future. Showing them your roadmap will reassure them that you know where you're going and have a plan to get there.

Shifting Your Perspective

It's natural to want more independence as you grow older and to view household rules, like curfews and chores, as rigid and confining. However, structure and rules are an integral part of life, even for older adults.

Parents and other trusted adults are here to guide and support you as you build habits that will serve you well in many areas of life. These habits help you grow, succeed, and handle more responsibility over time.

Instead of seeing your parents as opponents trying to make your life difficult, try viewing them as valuable resources who are here to help you. They have a wealth of real-life experience that you can learn from.

If you see your parents, grandparents, or any trusted adult in your life as sources of wisdom instead of threats to your independence, you will be all the richer for it. Their life experiences are gifts you can tap into as you create your roadmap and chart your course.

Set Your Destination

The first step in developing a roadmap is to set a destination by envisioning what you want your life to look like within a specific timeframe. You could choose the end of the semester, the school year or even four years from now.

Dream big, but know the difference between dreams and fantasies. Whatever you choose will require real action and hard work rather than crossing your fingers and hoping things work out. Have fun and play with it. It's all a creation, and you're the architect.

Why a Roadmap Works

You might be thinking, "This is silly. I'm just making stuff up. It's not going to happen." But once you know what you stand for and where you want to go, you've set your course.

Your roadmap gives you direction. When friends pressure you to do something that doesn't feel right, you know where you stand and recognize when someone or something is pulling you off course.

You know what moves you forward, and who and what are holding you back. When you make a mistake and miss a turn, you can always use your roadmap to find your way again.

Bringing Your Vision to Life

Create → Ask → Do (CAD)

CAD is a straightforward framework for bringing your vision to life.

1. CREATE your vision

Picture the future you want. Imagine yourself already living it, and write it down in clear, specific detail, using the present tense.

Example: "I am a straight-A student who leads the student council and volunteers every week at the animal shelter."

2. ASK yourself questions

What qualities do I need to become that person?

What actions would I be taking?

What would I be doing?

3. DO the work

Start taking those actions. They become the stepping stones to your goals, and your goals lead you to your vision.

My Real-Life Example

While I only recently created the *CAD Framework (Create, Ask, Do)*, I realized it's something I've been using all along, without realizing it had a name. Here's how it showed up for me in high school:

CREATE:

At my eighth-grade graduation, my math teacher said, "If you keep getting A's, you might be the high school valedictorian." I didn't even know what a valedictorian was at the time, but once I looked it up, I created that as my vision.

ASK:

When I asked myself what qualities I needed, I picked:

- Determination
- Persistence
- Time management
- Strong study habits

DO:

I identified my action steps:

- Avoid procrastination
- Turn in assignments on time
- Go for extra help
- Study for tests

I stuck with it; I studied hard, wrote down all assignments, stayed focused, and asked for help when I needed it. It was hard work, but in the end, I became valedictorian. But even if I hadn't, I would have gone further than if I hadn't tried at all.

You won't always reach your goals. Your vision might shift, and that's okay. Developing new habits, staying focused, and taking small steps toward your destination is what counts.

Try This:

Take a moment to consider where you want to be in a few years.

- *What kind of life do you want to create?*

There's no correct answer. Just pick a direction that feels right for you. It could be to:

- *Graduate*
- *Start a business*
- *Travel*
- *Create a piece of art*
- *Help people*
- *Earn your own money*

Choose whatever speaks to you.

Now zoom in.

What qualities do you need to have?

What's one small move you can make this month that points you that way?

CHAPTER 22

SELF-CARE

Self-care is important for your overall well-being. Here are some simple practices to try:

- **Meditation** – Helps calm your mind and lowers your stress level. Meditating even for five quiet minutes a day can make a difference.

- **Breathing exercises** – Try inhaling for four seconds, holding briefly, and exhaling for four seconds. Repeat a few times to relax your body and mind.

- **Thirty-minute movement routine** – Whether it's a walk, yoga, dancing, or a quick bodyweight workout, it counts.

- **Upgrade your eating habits** – Hydrate. Add some color to your plate. Fuel your body with foods that help you feel good, not sluggish.

Start with small steps. Pick one or two things that make you feel better mentally, physically, and emotionally. Don't do it because I said so or because your parents want you to. Do it because you're choosing to take care of yourself.

Movement Over Exercise

Former First Lady Michelle Obama chose the perfect name for her national health campaign: *Let's Move!* While the program promoted healthy eating and physical activity for kids, the title focused on fun and natural ways for kids to be active and feel good.[47]

Movement can be anything:

- Stretching when you wake up

- Dancing around your room

- Playing basketball with a friend

- Taking a walk while listening to music

- Even just standing up and shaking out your body for two minutes

Move in a way that feels good to you. Your body was designed to move, and when you do, your energy shifts, your stress levels lower, and your mindset becomes lighter.

When Daily Practices Don't Work

If you're experiencing persistent feelings of sadness or hopelessness, withdrawing from friends or activities, changes in eating or sleeping habits, anxiety, or thoughts of suicide or self-harm, talk to your parents, guardian, or a trusted adult to get immediate help.

Don't hesitate to call 988, the Suicide & Crisis Lifeline. They can help connect you to the mental health services that best fit your needs.

Getting mental health services and talking to a therapist or psychiatrist doesn't mean you're weak. It demonstrates that you have the courage and strength to get the help you need to become your best self.

CHAPTER 23

IT'S YOUR TIME

Walt Disney's line, "Keep moving forward," is something I often repeat silently to myself, and I remind others to do as well. Put one foot in front of the other and keep going.

You won't always move forward, and that's okay. What matters is that moving forward remains your goal. Sometimes you'll move backward. That's part of life. Have you ever heard the saying *"two steps forward and one step back,"* or watched a football player or basketball player take a few steps back before running ahead to win the game?

Sometimes you need to take a step back to learn something, rest, or even change direction. There is nothing wrong with stepping back, just as long as you don't stay there. Don't pressure yourself to have every detail figured out. You don't need a perfect plan. You need to start, take action, and keep moving forward the best way you can. This is your life, your journey, and your time. Let your light shine for all the world to see.

PART IV:
AMPLIFYING YOUTH VOICES AND
UNLOCKING POTENTIAL

CHAPTER 24

LEADING TOGETHER—YOUTH VOICE IN AC-TION ON THE LOCAL LEVEL

S o far, we've discussed ways to rebuild trust and restore connec-tion on an individual level. I've also provided young people with strategies to navigate life's challenges as they strive to be the best versions of themselves.

Now we will zoom out to the organizational level. This chapter, as well as the next, will explore what happens when young people not only speak up but step into leadership, help shape policy, and take their place at the decision-making table.

The tone might feel a little different since it's more about systems and institutions, but it's still about trusting youth and creating space for their voices to matter. We often describe young people as "future leaders." The intention is good, but it implies they're not ready yet. As demonstrated in Chapter 3, young people have made significant contributions by serving as leaders in schools, communities, and on global stages.

What if we partnered with youth now rather than in the future? Im-agine combining their energy, creativity, technological expertise, and empathy with our knowledge and real-world experience. We could step outside the confines of what we've always done and walk hand in hand with youth to create something new that shifts the trajectory of our planet.

Across the country and around the globe, young people are stepping into power, not just as individual changemakers, but as part of organizations that shape policy, transform systems, and hold institutions accountable.

In Boston, high school students on the Boston Student Advisory Council have influenced district-wide policies on student rights, discipline, and equity. They organize, sit with decision-makers, and help rewrite the rules that govern their schools.[48]

In New Jersey, the NJAAP Youth Advisory Committee is showing what it means to lead in the realm of public health. These young leaders are co-creating mental health resources, shaping statewide health messaging, and ensuring that youth voices drive real change in medical systems that often overlook them.[49]

In 1995, voters established the San Francisco Youth Commission to advise the Mayor and the Board of Supervisors on laws and policies affecting young people. Seventeen youth between the ages of twelve and twenty-three serve on the commission and provide recommendations on all proposed laws that would impact youth before the board takes action.[50]

The Youth Power Coalition (YPC) in New York City is an intergenerational organization where power is shared among its members. Youth leaders and adult allies make decisions ranging from strategic direction to budgeting and hiring. This model serves as a reminder that true partnership is collaborative, with young people fully taking their seats at the table.[51]

These councils, advisory boards, and commissions serve as proof that when young people have real societal accountability, they make a positive impact and effect meaningful change.

The question is no longer, *"How do we prepare youth to lead some-day?"* The question is, *"How do we support youth as they lead today?"* If young people are already stepping up and making a difference, the next step is to examine how our systems can welcome their leadership.

CHAPTER 25

EXPANDING YOUTH VOICE

❤❤❤

What if we expanded youth leadership on a national level and even a global level? There are some examples of this happening around the world.

Canada provides a great example of how youth can work directly with the government to shape policy. The Prime Minister's Youth Council (PMYC) advises the Prime Minister, Cabinet Ministers, and senior officials on issues such as immigration, climate action, youth mental health, housing, and other national concerns. They also provide input on the development of policies that include public health, affordability, and poverty reduction. The PMYC is a model of how youth can be essential partners in national governance.[52]

Around the world, young people are already leading movements and creating solutions to global issues. On a global level, seven Youth Climate Councils (YCCs) from a wide range of nations are part of the Youth Climate Council Global Alliance (YCCGA). Six councils operate at the national level, and one operates at the city level. These include councils in Denmark, Poland, the Netherlands, Ghana, Costa Rica, Uganda, and Brazil, each working to influence climate policy and elevate youth voices within government institutions.[53]

Reimagining Leadership Together

Imagine creating an international youth task force consisting of youth from around the world. These young people can discuss and exert change on global issues, such as climate change and world health, that affect their future.

If we permit ourselves to think creatively, we could integrate youth as advisors at the cabinet level or establish national departments dedicated solely to youth well-being. Thinking outside the box, what if we created a Department of Youth as a national agency dedicated to supporting youth in areas like education and mental health? Shall we dare to imagine having a Secretary of Youth Affairs in the Cabinet who is under the age of thirty? This young leader could play a pivotal role in shaping policies that impact the lives of young people and their future.

In some countries, this concept already exists to a certain extent. Portugal, for example, has a Secretary of State for Youth and Sports, a government position focused on youth development and policy.[54] But even there, that role is typically held by older adults—well-intentioned, but generations removed from the experiences of today's youth.

The above suggestions encourage people to challenge outdated ways of thinking and create something new that addresses the issues we face today. Just because we've always done it this way doesn't mean we should continue to do so. We can design systems and make policies with young people at the forefront of our decision-making, rather than an afterthought.

We can incorporate youth voice and leadership into every aspect of society, including business, media, education, and healthcare. When we collaborate with youth and embed their priorities with our own, they help shape the world we live in.

Why This Matters

Adults still have a critical role to play as mentors, allies, and system builders, but we must collaborate with the generations whose future is most at stake. It's about partnership, not control.

It's about building intergenerational teams that reflect the full range of experience, energy, and insight in our communities. It's about recognizing that young people bring new perspectives, especially when it comes to technology, mental health, identity, and the rapidly changing world they're inheriting.

It is not about lowering standards. It's about raising the standard for what inclusive, responsive leadership can look like.

And when done right, communities become stronger and institutions become more trusted. It's a win-win.

What Adults Can Do

You don't have to overhaul your system tomorrow. But you can start here:

- **Ask better questions.** Where do young people have a voice, and where don't they? Are they invited in after decisions are made, or while decisions are being shaped?

- **Remove barriers.** What's preventing youth from fully participating—age, access, culture, or language?

- **Reflect on power.** Who do you trust to lead? And why? Are you open to being challenged and changed by new perspectives?

- **Bring youth in.** Not just as guests or interns, but as co-creators with real influence.

- **Show them how it works.** Teach the systems and the unwritten rules so that they can lead with understanding.

- **Offer mentorship.** And be open to learning in return.

- **Compensate their time.** Respect youth contributions as real labor, not volunteer work.

- **Be patient.** Youth leadership takes time, trust, and space to grow.

What Young People Can Do

- **Listen first.** Understand the history, context, and people who came before, not to agree with everything, but to lead with respect.

- **Acknowledge what works.** Not everything needs to be torn down. Some systems are worth preserving and improving.

- **Challenge what doesn't.** Speak up with courage when something is broken, harmful, or outdated.

- **Learn how systems work.** Not to conform but to navigate them, influence them, and when needed, transform them.

- **Ask for feedback.** Growth doesn't mean giving up your voice. It means strengthening it.

- **Practice compromise.** You can stay rooted in your values and still build bridges with others.

- **Be consistent.** Change takes time. Keep showing up even when the process is slow or imperfect.

Transformation isn't about starting over. It's about knowing what's worth keeping, letting go of what no longer helps, and creating what's missing. That's how change happens in ourselves, our communities, and our world.

So the question isn't, *"Are young people ready to lead?"* The question is, *"Are we ready to lead with them?"*

CHAPTER 26

IT TAKES ALL OF US

Youth need to be grounded and connected. Not every young person has a traditional family. Some have parents who are absent, overworked, or overwhelmed. Some are raised by a grandparent, an older sibling, or an aunt. Others are in foster care or moving from one temporary place to another. That's exactly why the community matters so much.

When family is unavailable, the community must step in to provide support. Churches, schools, after-school programs, coaches, mentors, neighbors—these are the people who can connect.

The Promise of Adolescence states, "If provided with the proper supports and protection, normal processes of growth and maturation can lead youth to form healthy relationships with their peers and families, develop a sense of identity and self, and experience enriching and memorable engagements with the world."[55] Whether it's immediate family, extended relatives, or a chosen community, what matters most is connection.

We can't keep saying, "That's not my child." We need to look out for one another. Each and every one of us is a spark—a source of connection, care, and change.

Young people thrive when they feel supported and recognized as valuable contributors to their communities. And when they thrive, we all thrive.

CHAPTER 27

THE NEXT STEP

Small daily action steps can transform how we connect, lead, and grow together. Remember to use the SPARK Connection Framework as your guide.

- **S**upport each other without trying to fix or control anyone or anything.

- **P**resence means putting away distractions and being fully attentive.

- **A**uthenticity is speaking truthfully.

- **R**esponsiveness is acting with care, even in the smallest of ways.

- **K**nowing is looking beyond the surface by seeing others for who they truly are, and taking time to know yourself.

Receive a free guide to help you take action today by going to: https://www.drlizconsulting.com/spark/

ABOUT THE AUTHOR

Dr. Elizabeth R. Henry, widely known as Dr. Liz, is an Ivy League–trained, board-certified pediatrician, bestselling author, international speaker, and consultant who empowers parents, educators, and organizations to better support teens and young adults. With more than 25 years of experience, she delivers clear, practical strategies to strengthen communication, reduce conflict, and build the confidence and life skills young people need to thrive.

A graduate of Princeton University, the Perelman School of Medicine at the University of Pennsylvania, and Georgetown University's Pediatric Residency Program, Dr. Liz blends rigorous medical training with a compassionate, insightful approach to adolescent development, communication, and emotional well-being.

As founder and CEO of Dr. Liz Consulting, she equips parents, educators, youth-serving professionals, and young people themselves with tools to foster connection, resilience, and mental wellness. A TEDx speaker and trusted media voice, Dr. Liz has partnered with leading institutions, including PepsiCo, Bank of America, Kean University, SUNY Purchase College, and the Congressional Caucus on Black Women and Girls, to deliver impactful programs focused on youth engagement and emotional growth. She has also been featured in major media outlets, including as a frequent contributor for CBS News New York.

She lives in New Jersey with her husband and is the proud mother of a daughter in her twenties. A lifelong Girl Scout and active member of Alpha Kappa Alpha Sorority, Inc. and The National Drifters, Inc., Dr.

Liz enjoys watching movies, attending Broadway shows, and supporting the arts in her free time.

Her first book, *You Are Not a Bad Parent*, was a #1 Amazon bestseller and offers a proven, compassionate guide for navigating the challenges of parenting through adolescence and early adulthood.

NOTES

[1] "WISQARS Leading Causes of Death Visualization Tool," *Centers for Disease Control and Prevention*, https://wisqars.cdc.gov/lcd/, accessed July 19, 2025.

[2] Substance Abuse and Mental Health Services Administration, *Key Substance Use and Mental Health Indicators in the United States: Results from the 2023 National Survey on Drug Use and Health* (HHS Publication No. PEP24-07-021, NSDUH Series H-59) (Rockville, MD: Center for Behavioral Health Statistics and Quality, 2024), https://www.samhsa.gov/data/report/2023-nsduh-annual-national-report.

[3] Centers for Disease Control and Prevention, *Youth Risk Behavior Survey Data Summary & Trends Report: 2013–2023* (Washington, DC: U.S. Department of Health and Human Services, 2024).

[4] R. Nath et al., *2024 U.S. National Survey on the Mental Health of LGBTQ+ Young People* (West Hollywood, CA: The Trevor Project, 2024), https://www.thetrevorproject.org/survey-2024.

[5] National Center for Health Statistics, "Percentage of Teens Aged 12–17 Years with Symptoms of Depression during the Past 2 Weeks, United States, July 2021–December 2023," *National Health Interview Survey—Teen*, generated July 19, 2025, https://wwwn.cdc.gov/NHISDataQueryTool/NHIS_teen/index.html

[6] Thea L. Anderson et al., "Contributing Factors to the Rise in Adolescent Anxiety and Associated Mental Health Disorders: A Narrative Review of Current Literature," *Journal of Child and Adolescent Psychiatric Nursing* 38, no. 1 (2024): e70009, https://doi.org/10.1111/jcap.70009.

[7] Substance Abuse and Mental Health Services Administration, Key Substance Use and Mental Health Indicators in the United States: Results from the 2024 National Survey on Drug Use and Health, HHS Publication No. PEP25-07-007, NSDUH Series H-60 (Center for Behavioral Health Statistics and Quality, Substance Abuse and Mental Health Services Administration, 2025), https://www.samhsa.gov/data/report/2024-nsduh-annual-national-report

[8] Office of the Surgeon General (U.S.), *Protecting Youth Mental Health: The U.S. Surgeon General's Advisory* (Washington, DC: U.S. Department of Health and Human Services, 2021), https://www.hhs.gov/sites/default/files/surgeon-general-youth-mental-health-advisory.pdf, accessed July 19, 2025.

[9] American Academy of Pediatrics, American Academy of Child and Adolescent Psychiatry, and Children's Hospital Association, *AAP-AACAP-CHA Declaration of a National Emergency in Child and Adolescent Mental Health* (Itasca, IL: American Academy of Pediatrics, 2021), https://www.aap.org/en/advocacy/child-and-adolescent-healthy-mental-development/aap-aacap-cha-declaration-of-a-national-emergency-in-child-and-adolescent-mental-health/, accessed July 19, 2025.

[10] "Are Major Natural Disasters Increasing?" *USAFacts*, https://usafacts.org/articles/are-the-number-of-major-natural-disasters-increasing/, accessed July 19, 2025.

[11] "Are Major Natural Disasters Increasing?" *USAFacts*.

[12] National Academies of Sciences, Engineering, and Medicine, *The Promise of Adolescence: Realizing Opportunity for All Youth* (Washington, DC: The National Academies Press, 2019), 27, https://doi.org/10.17226/25388.

[13] Kim Parker, "How Pew Research Center Will Report on Generations Moving Forward," *Pew Research Center*, May 22, 2023,

https://www.pewresearch.org/short-reads/2023/05/22/how-pew-research-center-will-report-on-generations-moving-forward/.

[14] Michael Dimock, "Defining Generations: Where Millennials End and Generation Z Begins," *Pew Research Center*, January 17, 2019, https://www.pewresearch.org/short-reads/2019/01/17/where-millennials-end-and-generation-z-begins/.

[15] Ralph Ryback, "From Baby Boomers to Generation Z," *Psychology Today*, February 22, 2016, https://www.psychologytoday.com/us/blog/the-truisms-of-wellness/201602/from-baby-boomers-to-generation-z.

[16] Ryback, "From Baby Boomers to Generation Z."

[17] Dimock, "Defining Generations: Where Millennials End and Generation Z Begins."

[18] Ryback, "From Baby Boomers to Generation Z."

[19] Kim Parker, Nikki Graf, and Ruth Igielnik, "Generation Z Looks a Lot Like Millennials on Key Social and Political Issues," *Pew Research Center*, January 17, 2019, https://www.pewresearch.org/social-trends/2019/01/17/generation-z-looks-a-lot-like-millennials-on-key-social-and-political-issues/.

[20] John Della Volpe, *Fight: How Gen Z Is Channeling Their Fear and Passion to Save America*, 1st ed. (New York: St. Martin's Press, 2022), 136, 166.

[21] Mark McCrindle and Ashley Fell, *Understanding Generation Alpha* (Sydney: McCrindle Research Pty Ltd, 2020), https://generationalpha.com/wp-content/uploads/2020/02/Understanding-Generation-Alpha-McCrindle.pdf.

[22] Parker, "How Pew Research Center Will Report on Generations Moving Forward."

[23] "Malala's Story," *Malala Fund*, 2025, https://malala.org/malalas-story, accessed July 20, 2025.

[24] "Malala's Story," *Malala Fund*, 2025.

[25] "Malala Yousafzai – Facts," *NobelPrize.org*, Nobel Prize Outreach, 2025, https://www.nobelprize.org/prizes/peace/2014/yousafzai/facts/, accessed July 20, 2025.

[26] Charlotte Alter, "How Parkland Teens Are Leading the Gun Control Conversation," *TIME*, March 22, 2018, https://time.com/5205938/never-again-movement/, accessed July 20, 2025.

[27] *March For Our Lives*, 2025, https://marchforourlives.org/, accessed July 20, 2025.

[28] Della Volpe, *Fight*, pp. 70–76.

[29] *March For Our Lives*, https://marchforourlives.org/.

[30] Marley Dias, "About," *Marley Dias*, 2025, https://www.marleydias.com/about/, accessed July 20, 2025.

[31] Marley Dias, "About."

[32] TIME Staff, "Kid of the Year: Meet Gitanjali Rao," *TIME*, December 3, 2020, https://time.com/5916772/kid-of-the-year-2020/, accessed July 20, 2025.

[33] Gitanjali Rao, "Profile," *Gitanjali Rao*, 2023, https://gitanjalirao.net/profile, accessed July 20, 2025.

[34] Sir Darius Brown, "About Sir Darius," *Sir Darius Brown*, 2025, https://sirdariusbrown.com/pages/about-sir-darius, accessed July 20, 2025.

[35] Sir Darius Brown, "About Sir Darius."

36 Ryan Hickman, "About Ryan's Recycling," *Ryan's Recycling*, 2025, https://ryansrecycling.com/about/, accessed July 20, 2025.

37 Hickman, "About Ryan's Recycling."

38 National Academies of Sciences, *The Promise of Adolescence*, 46-59

39 National Academies of Sciences, *The Promise of Adolescence*, 19

40 National Academies of Sciences, *The Promise of Adolescence*, 75

41 National Academies of Sciences, *The Promise of Adolescence*, 70-71

42 CNN Staff, "Florida Student Emma Gonzalez to Lawmakers and Gun Advocates: 'We Call BS,'" *CNN*, last modified February 17, 2018, https://www.cnn.com/2018/02/17/us/florida-student-emma-gonzalez-speech.

43 *The Matrix*, directed by Lana Wachowski and Lilly Wachowski (Burbank, CA: Warner Bros., 1999), film.

44 "Malala's Story," *Malala Fund*, 2025.

45 "Malala's Story," *Malala Fund*, 2025.

46 *We Bought a Zoo*, directed by Cameron Crowe (Los Angeles: 20th Century Fox, 2011), film.

47 *Let's Move!*, archived at Obama White House Archives, accessed July 20, 2025, https://letsmove.obamawhitehouse.archives.gov/.

48 Boston Public Schools, *Boston Student Advisory Council (BSAC)*, accessed July 20, 2025, https://www.bostonpublicschools.org/bps-departments/opportunity-youth/bsac.

[49] New Jersey Chapter, American Academy of Pediatrics. *Youth Advisory Committee (YAC)*. Accessed July 20, 2025. https://njaap.org/yac/.

[50] City and County of San Francisco. *Youth Commission*. Accessed July 20, 2025. https://www.sfgov.org/youthcommission/.

[51] Youth Power Coalition. *Youth Power Coalition*. Accessed July 20, 2025. https://www.youthpowercoalition.org/.

[52] Government of Canada. *Members in Action – Prime Minister's Youth Council*. Last modified June 3, 2025. Accessed July 20, 2025. https://www.canada.ca/en/campaign/prime-ministers-youth-council/members-in-action.html.

[53] weADAPT. *Creating Youth Climate Councils: A Step-by-Step Guide for Young People*. Accessed July 20, 2025. https://weadapt.org/knowledge-base/cities-and-climate-change/creating-youth-climate-councils-a-step-by-step-guide-for-young-people/.

[54] European Education and Culture Executive Agency. *1.4 Youth Policy Decision-Making – Portugal*. Last updated November 28, 2023. Accessed July 20, 2025. https://national-policies.eacea.ec.europa.eu/youthwiki/chapters/portugal/14-youth-policy-decision-making.

[55] National Academies of Sciences, *The Promise of Adolescence*, 75

BIBLIOGRAPHY

American Academy of Pediatrics, American Academy of Child and Adolescent Psychiatry, and Children's Hospital Association. *AAP-AACAP-CHA Declaration of a National Emergency in Child and Adolescent Mental Health*. Itasca, IL: American Academy of Pediatrics, 2021. https://www.aap.org/en/advocacy/child-and-adolescent-healthy-mental-development/aap-aacap-cha-declaration-of-a-national-emergency-in-child-and-adolescent-mental-health/. Accessed July 19, 2025.

Anderson, Thea L., et al. "Contributing Factors to the Rise in Adolescent Anxiety and Associated Mental Health Disorders: A Narrative Review of Current Literature." *Journal of Child and Adolescent Psychiatric Nursing* 38, no. 1 (2024): e70009. https://doi.org/10.1111/jcap.70009.

Boston Public Schools. *Boston Student Advisory Council (BSAC)*. Accessed July 20, 2025. https://www.bostonpublicschools.org/bps-departments/opportunity-youth/bsac.

Brown, Sir Darius. "About Sir Darius." *Sir Darius Brown*. 2025. https://sirdariusbrown.com/pages/about-sir-darius. Accessed July 20, 2025.

Centers for Disease Control and Prevention. *Youth Risk Behavior Survey Data Summary & Trends Report: 2013–2023*. Washington, DC: U.S. Department of Health and Human Services, 2024.

CNN Staff. "Florida Student Emma Gonzalez to Lawmakers and Gun Advocates: 'We Call BS.'" *CNN*. Last modified February 17, 2018. https://www.cnn.com/2018/02/17/us/florida-student-emma-gonzalez-speech.

City and County of San Francisco. *Youth Commission*. Accessed July 20, 2025. https://www.sfgov.org/youthcommission/.

Della Volpe, John. *Fight: How Gen Z Is Channeling Their Fear and Passion to Save America*. 1st ed. New York: St. Martin's Press, 2022.

Dimock, Michael. "Defining Generations: Where Millennials End and Generation Z Begins." *Pew Research Center*. January 17, 2019. https://www.pewresearch.org/short-reads/2019/01/17/where-millennials-end-and-generation-z-begins/.

European Education and Culture Executive Agency. *1.4 Youth Policy Decision-Making – Portugal*. Last updated November 28, 2023. Accessed July 20, 2025. https://national-policies.eacea.ec.europa.eu/youthwiki/chapters/portugal/14-youth-policy-decision-making.

Government of Canada. *Members in Action – Prime Minister's Youth Council*. Last modified June 3, 2025. Accessed July 20, 2025. https://www.canada.ca/en/campaign/prime-ministers-youth-council/members-in-action.html.

Hickman, Ryan. "About Ryan's Recycling." *Ryan's Recycling*. 2025. https://ryansrecycling.com/about/. Accessed July 20, 2025.

Malala Fund. "Malala's Story." 2025. https://malala.org/malalas-story. Accessed July 20, 2025.

March For Our Lives. 2025. https://marchforourlives.org/. Accessed July 20, 2025.

McCrindle, Mark, and Ashley Fell. *Understanding Generation Alpha.* Sydney: McCrindle Research Pty Ltd, 2020. https://generationalpha.com/wp-content/uploads/2020/02/Understanding-Generation-Alpha-McCrindle.pdf.

National Academies of Sciences, Engineering, and Medicine. *The Promise of Adolescence: Realizing Opportunity for All Youth.* Washington, DC: The National Academies Press, 2019. https://doi.org/10.17226/25388.

National Center for Health Statistics. "Percentage of Teens Aged 12–17 Years with Symptoms of Depression during the Past 2 Weeks, United States, July 2021–December 2023." *National Health Interview Survey—Teen.* Generated July 19, 2025. https://wwwn.cdc.gov/NHISDataQueryTool/NHIS_teen/index.html

NJ Chapter, American Academy of Pediatrics. *Youth Advisory Committee (YAC).* Accessed July 20, 2025. https://njaap.org/yac/.

Office of the Surgeon General (U.S.). *Protecting Youth Mental Health: The U.S. Surgeon General's Advisory.* Washington, DC: U.S. Department of Health and Human Services, 2021. https://www.hhs.gov/sites/default/files/surgeon-general-youth-mental-health-advisory.pdf. Accessed July 19, 2025.

Parker, Kim. "How Pew Research Center Will Report on Generations Moving Forward." *Pew Research Center.* May 22, 2023. https://www.pewresearch.org/short-reads/2023/05/22/how-pew-research-center-will-report-on-generations-moving-forward/.

Parker, Kim, Nikki Graf, and Ruth Igielnik. "Generation Z Looks a Lot Like Millennials on Key Social and Political Issues." *Pew Research Center*. January 17, 2019. https://www.pewresearch.org/social-trends/2019/01/17/generation-z-looks-a-lot-like-millennials-on-key-social-and-political-issues/.

Rao, Gitanjali. "Profile." *Gitanjali Rao*. 2023. https://gitanjali-rao.net/profile. Accessed July 20, 2025.

Ryback, Ralph. "From Baby Boomers to Generation Z." *Psychology Today*. February 22, 2016. https://www.psychologytoday.com/us/blog/the-truisms-of-wellness/201602/from-baby-boomers-to-generation-z.

Substance Abuse and Mental Health Services Administration. *Key Substance Use and Mental Health Indicators in the United States: Results from the 2023 National Survey on Drug Use and Health*. HHS Publication No. PEP24-07-021, NSDUH Series H-59. Rockville, MD: Center for Behavioral Health Statistics and Quality, 2024. https://www.samhsa.gov/data/report/2023-nsduh-annual-national-report.

Substance Abuse and Mental Health Services Administration. Key Substance Use and Mental Health Indicators in the United States: Results from the 2024 National Survey on Drug Use and Health. HHS Publication No. PEP25-07-007, NSDUH Series H-60. Center for Behavioral Health Statistics and Quality, Substance Abuse and Mental Health Services Administration, 2025. https://www.samhsa.gov/data/report/2024-nsduh-annual-national-report

The Trevor Project. R. Nath et al. *2024 U.S. National Survey on the Mental Health of LGBTQ+ Young People*. West Hollywood, CA: The Trevor Project, 2024. https://www.thetrevorproject.org/survey-2024.

Time Staff. "Kid of the Year: Meet Gitanjali Rao." *TIME*, December 3, 2020. https://time.com/5916772/kid-of-the-year-2020/. Accessed July 20, 2025.

USAFacts. "Are Major Natural Disasters Increasing?" *USAFacts*. Updated July 7, 2025. https://usafacts.org/articles/are-the-number-of-major-natural-disasters-increasing/. Accessed July 19, 2025.

We Bought a Zoo. Directed by Cameron Crowe. Los Angeles: 20th Century Fox, 2011. Film.

WISQARS. *WISQARS Leading Causes of Death Visualization Tool*. Centers for Disease Control and Prevention. https://wisqars.cdc.gov/lcd/. Accessed July 19, 2025.

Youth Power Coalition. *Youth Power Coalition*. Accessed July 20, 2025. https://www.youthpowercoalition.org/.

WeADAPT. *Creating Youth Climate Councils: A Step-by-Step Guide for Young People*. Accessed July 20, 2025. https://weadapt.org/knowledge-base/cities-and-climate-change/creating-youth-climate-councils-a-step-by-step-guide-for-young-people/.

www.ingramcontent.com/pod-product-compliance
Lightning Source LLC
Chambersburg PA
CBHW052140270326
41930CB00012B/2961